CREED

Lee Robinson

Plain View Press
P. O. 42255
Austin, TX 78704

plainviewpress.net
sb@plainviewpress.net
1-512-441-2452

Copyright Lee Robinson 2009. All rights reserved.
ISBN: 978-0-911051-76-6
Library of Congress Number: 2009920239

Cover art *Monstrous Regiment Of Women* by Jacob Rickard.

Acknowledgments

I am grateful to the editors of the following magazines, journals and anthologies, where these poems first appeared, sometimes in slightly different form: "A Citizen's Response to the Pamphlet Distributed by the U.S. Department of Homeland Security" and "1-800-RU-n-PAIN" in *Texas Observer*; "Advice We Give Our Children" in *South Carolina Poetry Society Yearbook*; "Being There" and "Silk" in *The Southern Poetry Anthology, Vol. I*, ed. Stephen Gardner and William Wright, Texas Review Press, 2007; "Cooking with Leftovers" in *Rattapallax*; "Creed" in *Kalliope* (Finalist, 2005 Sue Elkind Prize); "Floater" in *Southern Poetry Review*; "Hold On" in *San Antonio Express-News*; "The Logic of Last Monday Night" in *Harper's Magazine*; "The Night Toboggan" in *You, Year: New Poems from Point Poets*, ed. Thomas Johnson, Harbinger Publications, 1996; "No Counting" in *Kakalak Poetry Anthology 2006*; "Reversal" in *Main Street Rag*; and "Snow" in *Appalachia*.

for Max and Vic

Contents

Invitation   7

I.

Before Words   11
No Counting   13
Hold On   15
Labor   16
The Logic of Last Monday Night   18
A Curriculum in Dreams   19
Feeding the Children   21
The Goldberg Variations   22
Silk   24
Second Marriage   26
Cooking With Leftovers   27
Being There   29
News from the Underground   31

II.

The Man Who Sold Us the Farm   35
A Citizen's Response to the Pamphlet Distributed by the
    U.S. Department of Homeland Security   36
Instructions for Contact in Case of Emergency   37
Country Equity   38
A Second Coming   40
Thanksgiving   41
Midsummer in the Blue Ridge   42
Equinox   44

III.

The Gift   47
The Night Toboggan   48
Snow   50
On the Road   51
Fireflies   52
In That Other World   53
Remembering the Parrot of Carolina   54
Verge of Extinction   55

5

Floater	56
Rising	58
Drought	59
Reversal	60
Red	61

IV.

My Father As Zookeeper	65
Menopause	66
In the Country of the Young	67
Advice We Give Our Children	68
His Father	69
The Lions	70
Looking Out	71
Coquinas	72
Television	73
1-800-RU-n-PAIN	74
Black Friday	75
This Body	76
The Loop	77
Prayer	78
Understudy	79
To the Young Man of Middle Eastern Descent at Gate 13, London to New York	80
Creed	81
Notes	82
About the Author	83

Invitation

Shall we begin, you and I, two
   strangers finding each other nose to
     nose in the nook of the page, in the breath
        between words, the moment when

the words, having some time ago been
   put to bed, come awake at your touch?
     Okay, you say, *but we can't exactly be*
       equal partners in this affair. I hear you,

and though I make no promises, I already
   love you for your outspokenness. Come: I can't
     do this without you—your doubts and your
       indulgences, your hand turning

the page, taking mine. I lean on you,
   you lean on me. We could dance like this
     for hours. I sing the lyrics in your ear, you hum
       the melody: *the book's not mine, but ours.*

I.

Before Words

      for Jonah

Shadow, I say, and point
to the shape of your small hand
on the sidewalk.

You close your fist, then open it.
Shadow, I say again. *See how it changes
when you move?* This is your first

October in the light.
You bring your hand to your face,
searching each finger

for the source of such magical power.
Later there'll be time to explain how a body
blocks the sun, for the story of our sailing

around a dying star and how
our tilting on an invisible axis
will bring your second summer.

There will be time for all of that and more,
enough for me to tell you
how we came to be a kind of kin,

to trace the lineage— your father's father
leaving the hills of Chiang Mai
for America, your mother's great-grandmother,

nine years old, fleeing the shtetl
and stepping alone
onto the streets of Manhattan.

Continued

And though the blood that sings in your fingers
has none of mine, I can try, if you ask,
to explain how sometimes people fall out of love,

how sometimes they leave each other,
how you came to have three grandmothers.
I can draw the lines that bring you here,

to South Texas,
where we watch the shape of your hand
move across the sidewalk. *Shadow*, I say,

but you see something beyond words,
you hear in the rustle of wind in the trees
what we cannot speak;

among the falling leaves you find
what we always knew before
we had a word for it. I see it in your eyes.

Your hand follows mine, our fingers
closing, opening: shadows
of starfish, shadows of stars.

No Counting

Of birthdays this is my sixtieth,
of months this is the first, of days the fourth,
of years two thousand eight in the Common Era.
Of eyes that are mine there are two, and they open
into the bedroom that is one of two in a house
I share with my second husband,
to whom I have been married nine years
of the total of thirty-seven I have spent as a wife.
Of children out in the world who were born to me
there are two, of which the man-child is thirty-three
and living in a city three thousand miles away
and the woman-child
is twenty nine and in her eighteenth year of school
in a city of eight million
seventeen hundred miles away.

Of things these children know nothing about
the stars are not as many, and of things they are sure about
there are even more. Of loves they have lain with
there have been fewer than ten (between the two of them)
disclosed to me but undoubtedly more, and pray more
until the right ones come along.
Of advice about love their requirement is infinite.
Of advice they want from me there is none.

Of years I worked in courtrooms there were twenty-five.
Of years I taught in classrooms, ten.
Of years that are left to me
there may be thirty if I am lucky
and if I am unlucky, as many as forty.
Of lives I have lived this is the only one I know of
and of lives I will live, I expect it is the last,
though if I were offered another I would take it, even if

Continued

of the hundreds of cedar waxwings flying
overhead this morning I were the one on the far edge
of the flock, the one closest to the hungry hawk,
and even if— especially if—
in the days I would live as a waxwing there would be
no counting.

Hold On

The cell phone in my hand's no bigger than
a baby bird. I cradle it and strain
to hear my daughter's voice, tonight beamed in
from her room in Brooklyn by way of heaven.
Our connection's fragile, begins to break;
Hold on, I say, and step outside—dusk now,
dim stars. Above my head barn swallows take
a meal of insects to the one who flew
a day or two too soon, then hit the ground.
(I picked it up, restored it to its nest.)
I ask about the job, the steady boyfriend.
We're breaking up, she says, *I think it's best.*
There's static now, she goes to the window,
my fledgling, who'll fly again tomorrow.

Labor

    i.

I thought I wouldn't live through it,
the pain coming at me mean as a fist,
pummeling again and again
until I gave up and begged
for the knock-out punch.

I closed my eyes
and tried to breathe as I'd been told
but the body (not mine anymore)
wouldn't listen, just
wanted to die.

I had almost forgotten what the torture
was for when I heard his cry.
Afterwards we lay together, each
reaching out
for the other survivor.

    ii.

A veteran by then, a bold
amnesiac, I volunteered a second time.
It was over before I knew it. I came home
with a girl, home to the house
I ran like a factory: up at night

to nurse and do the wash, up at dawn
to nurse again and pack the lunchbox, do
my turn at carpool, get to the office by nine.
Complaints ripened into boasts:
I was always "fine."

Each year I fattened the family purse—
husband, children, house—
counted my blessings
and did my best to forget
the looming deficit.

    iii.

And now, retired, I discover
the job's not over. This is the work
nobody trained me for, the surprise assignment
I can't turn down. No use asking
What for, I show up early every day,

dutifully punch the clock and sit
where I watch, from afar, the children at work
on their lives. They don't see me.
I'm the old supervisor
stripped of my power,

I watch and wait, as if my distant loving
can save them from suffering.
Good worker that I am, I try
to keep my mouth shut, learn to love
even this hard labor.

The Logic of Last Monday Night

At the end of the runway
the fetus kicked. My sister
is on that plane. Flames lick
at the edge of the electric
blanket and if I turn it off
maybe the cops will quit
their neighborhood drug raid
or whatever it is
they are up to out there,
red lights flashing.
My sister is on that plane,
but she left the day before,
already an aunt. This churning
in my gut, at least, is not a dream,
waking from its dream,
wanting out.

A Curriculum in Dreams

      i.

Sixth grade, I'm playing
softball, relieved
I've been picked for the team.
Amazing, how I seem to fit in,
my temporary wholesomeness
a palpable thing.
Outfield, I reach for the ball
that falls towards my glove
in delicious slow motion.
Then a scream: they turn to see me
naked, my feet frozen under me
so even my fastest running
gets me nowhere.

      ii.

I'm leading lady
in the college play
but no one's let me
see the script. And later
I'm about to be *cum laude*,
maybe even *magna*,
when the dean discovers
I'm lacking History 103.

      iii.

Those are the dreams I go back to so often
there's nostalgia in the horror,
but now at middle age I dream
the hidden room behind the door
only I can open. I wonder

Continued

how it could have been here all along,
undiscovered, in the house
I've lived in for twenty years, this room
with enormous windows
looking out to the sea.

I open the shutters, shedding
my fears one after another
like outgrown skins,
and there is nothing at all astonishing
about how I lift myself up,
away, with wings that unfold
from somewhere deep inside me.

Feeding the Children

They won't let me finish the dream of swimming
with porpoises in a turquoise sea, their cries
coming from far away, then near. I turn on the bed
that isn't a beach, remembering

I am their mother, put on robe and slippers,
make coffee in dawn's half light, turn the radio
to yesterday's casualty count: two MIA's, a stray
bomb in a Baghdad market, in Basra tiny bodies

crushed by the mob around the relief truck.
I burn the toast, scrape the blackened skin
into the garbage can, disguise its wounds
with butter but leave it on the plate when I go out.

I wonder if they have felt it already—
the son in London, six hours ahead,
the daughter in Eastern Standard—felt
the day clench against itself like an empty gut?

In the bare branches the cardinals dart impatiently.
Spreading their seed, I let myself believe they need me.

The Goldberg Variations

      for Sarah Steinhardt

I have listened over and over
and now I think I know why
you gave me this CD, why you wanted me

to hear the sound of Gould at 22, in 1955,
technically almost perfect, the *tour de force*
that would make him famous

and then the version played in '82—
just months before his stroke—
because, as he said, he could not identify

with the spirit of the person
who made the earlier recording.
But I think this second rendering

is not so altogether different
as he imagined it, not like
two different lives but more

the same life revising itself,
the same force
derived from the same old pulse

but felt now completely
because it is
so full of years.

You wanted me to hear
the young man's almost unbearable
energy, the older's tender fortitude,

feel the same spine curved over the keys,
the same hands moving, one constant
reference point in the music.

You wanted me to hear
these variations on variations,
the contrapuntal spirit,

the playfulness amid the utmost
seriousness, the childhood notes
that play and skip, then slow

to somber canon, things lost
and things that are not
what they seem.

You wanted me to hear Gould
as he tried to coax perfection
out of wood and string,

knowing (as he said)
there is no real climax,
never any resolution.

You gave me these variations
as if to say *Listen to me,*
listen to all the years of recitals,

the competitions, listen to the girl
who wanted to be famous,
the woman who earns a living

selling Steinways, giving lessons,
who gets up early every morning
to practice in the dark.

Silk

Imagine
you are in another country,
your guidebook
to this village
years out of date.
Dusty streets teem
with women in caftans,
their faces half-hidden, their eyes
never quite meeting yours.

You stumble on the market
and ask about the merchant
famous for his red silk,
but you get a blank look,
and when you ask again,
a sharp, *No English!*
Didn't the innkeeper
say he was here, or was that
another town?

You bump against bodies
going the other way, smelling
of sweat and spices; you come
full circle in the labyrinth of stalls:
strange fruits, birds and bats
in cages, a hundred bolts of cloth
but no silk.

Ignore the hands reaching out to you
with their cheap, rough goods.
Ignore the shouting, the pushing.
Keep going until you reach the end of town.
There you'll find the bench beside the sea
where sailboats float like butterflies.
Wait there.

Someone will come
who speaks your language, whose
boat takes you out to open water, out
where the village disappears and there is nothing
but the sea and the two of you
behind the billowing spinnaker—
the red sail full of the wind
and shimmering in the sun
like silk.

Second Marriage

Let us admit, this second time, there are
impediments. But love is not less which sees
its faults etched deep in time's unsteady mirror,
nor less because it bends on creaking knees
to mend the shattered glass with compromise.
Love isn't love which won't admit it's quick
to trip on baggage long forgot, nor wise
to lean too hard on pride's thin walking stick.
To this unvirgin coupling we'll invite
that bride and groom we wed another day—
RSVP, but no regrets. She'll sit
front row, he'll stand to give my heart away.
They'll trade their stories as we kiss, and smile
behind us as we stumble down the aisle.

Cooking With Leftovers

Take me now, before it's too late
is what it might say if it could speak,
this wedge of eggplant haphazardly wrapped
in a paper towel, looking up, bereft,
when I open the refrigerator for milk.

Okay, I agree, thinking something
might come of this, something elegant,
perhaps a ratatouille Provencale, but the recipe
calls for ingredients my cupboard lacks, so
I scrounge around in the vegetable bin, find
half an onion, a wrinkled portabello,
some spaghetti sauce I made last week,
a hunk of cheese (pock-marked with mold
but restored with only minor surgery)
and two gnarled yet pliable cloves of garlic.
Inspired, I pour a glass of wine (forget the milk!)
and turn the radio to oldies.

Carole King accompanies the chopping,
a slow sauté, garlic dancing in olive oil. I feel
the earth move under my feet, turn up the heat,
toss the onion in, then the eggplant
and the mushroom. All this into a baking dish,
the one with a chip on its shoulder
I bought at a garage sale for a quarter.
I pour the sauce— a jazzy ooze—then grate
the cheese, set the oven to 350, and bake.

You'll come in time for supper,
opening the kitchen door
to the smell of serendipity.
When you inquire
I'll make up a story

Continued

of a mythical Cuisine whose queen
is Aubergine, who rides to the ball
with the Lord of Leftovers
in a phantasmagorical casserole.
So, my darling, don't ask what's in it:
just close your eyes and eat.

Being There

Six a.m.,
I get up to pee, my feet
groping for the slippers
you gave me
that first Christmas
we were married—

moccasins
lined with sheepskin,
half a size too small
but stretched now
to the shape of my toes.

I move in the dark
across the old pine floor
as if on ice, careful
not to wake you.
Hands held out
to feel for furniture,

I find
the bathroom, feel
the bottom of the toilet
bump against my feet,
turn to sit, then fall
with all my freight
(half middle-age, half sleep)
into the pit you made
when you left the seat up.

I confess I cursed you,
your small sin looming large
as I wallowed in the darkness,
in the cold shock

Continued

of the unexpected,
and would have said something
this morning, something
about thoughtlessness
had I not stopped at the window
on the way back to the bed
and seen there, in the moonlight,
the doe, alone.

She saw me, too,
or sensed the shape of danger.
For a moment we both froze before
she raised the white flag of her tail
and disappeared.

I crawled in beside you,
sent up a kind of prayer
in praise of your steady snore,
your being there.

News from the Underground

Stop, I shout at the kitchen radio.
It's 6 a.m. in San Antonio, I'm still
in my nightgown, not quite awake.
I want him to turn back, this man
behind the voice, I want him to apologize
and say it's not confirmed, this news
from the Underground in London,
but his voice is firm, his calm delivery
a kind of cruelty.

How can he not know
my son is there? If he did, would he
go on and on about the people
emerging with bloodied heads,
about the ones still trapped below, the bus
in Russell Square with its roof blown off?
Would he say, and say again—
the voice now a little husky—

   It was never a question of if, but when—

I dial the number: busy, busy, busy.
Fear swells in me, enough to send a scream
across an ocean. Somehow I find the room
where the laptop waits in its innocence,
log on, scroll down until

   Dear All,
   We're hearing news of explosions on the trains.
   I'm fine. At work. Left early this morning for my commute.
   Cell phones are jammed. Love, Luke

Continued

The rest of the day I praise each ordinary happening:
the bitterness of coffee left too long in the pot,
the slosh of water in the watering can.
In the adamant heat of high summer
the crickets applaud the tentative revival
of the wilted fern.
Small things:
such sweetnesses.

II.

The Man Who Sold Us the Farm

It was late April, already hot,
and where he sat under the pecan tree
the shade was the opposite of energy,
something long ago burnt out.
He fanned himself with his cowboy hat,
the movement of his arm so slow
it seemed suspended in the humid air.
When we got out of our car
he struggled to stand,
kicked over his bottle of Jim Beam,
his giant trunk swaying back and forth,
the legs beneath it trembling.

Almost nothing he said that afternoon
was true. He knew the roof would leak,
knew the plumbing was bad, knew
the horses weren't thoroughbred
and snakes hid in the uncut grass.
I'll leave the Chevrolet, he said,
*nothing wrong with the motor
but I've lost the key.* The car stayed—
he kept his word on that—but no amount
of tinkering could get it started, and for months
it sat with its hood up rusting in the pasture.

Before we left he grinned as if he knew
something about us we didn't know ourselves.
If you can't be happy here, he said,
you can't be happy anywhere.

Truth or lie?
We bought the farm.

A Citizen's Response to the Pamphlet Distributed by the U.S. Department of Homeland Security

Bottled water,
if we must, but better
the good champagne that has sat
undrunk too long on the wine rack.
From the pantry,
canned tomato soup and hearts
of artichoke, both palatable
when cold, and from the soon-to-be
powerless refrigerator, some leftover
morsels of brie and salami, both past
their expiration dates for safe consumption.

A flashlight? Instead
let's have candles for this feast.
No radio, but batteries for the boom box
and a few CD's—
Beethoven's Ninth, Willie Nelson,
Yellow Submarine.

Never mind
the duct tape and the plastic.
We'll open the windows or picnic
under the stars, taking deep
breaths, taking in
the smell of the prairie,
listening to the armadillo
rooting for ants,
and if we survive
until morning, the raucous boast
of the kingfisher
rising from the creek.

Instructions for Contact in Case of Emergency

Let me say this now
to avoid the agony
of busy signals and blank
computer screens:

Children,
stay where you are.
Celebrate your cities—
London, Miami,
San Antonio, New York.
Recite a poem
you can't live without
and something
from the Bill of Rights.
Sing all the songs you learned
on long car trips and some
you improvise.
Make love.

Husband,
you know where to come.
You know the combination to the gate
and how to drive up to the house
in the dark, looking out
for deer, avoiding the place
where the hundred-year flood
took a chunk of the road.
Come quickly:

Out here
there's plenty of sky
and the night
is still young.

Country Equity

There's no denying the cows
belong to my neighbor, the dairyman,
and so, the logic goes, their excrement—
but when I drive by his pasture

I can't help coveting them,
these uncountable mounds.
I close my eyes and see
spring rains filling his fields,

water rising around the soft brown
hills of turds until they give in
and slide into the swollen creek.
Wouldn't that be a kind of crime,

such waste of waste?
My spring garden's not yet tilled
but already I imagine
my trespass by the light of the moon,

my shovel and my plastic garbage bags,
the county sheriff with his spotlight
on my larceny— but I know my neighbor
wouldn't call the law.

He's a straightforward man, old
German stock, up at six to plow
and put his stone walls straight,
who not until his seventies could bring himself

to close the dairy down. (*No use*, he said,
trying to compete with the big boys anymore.)
If I ask him why he still rides out on his tractor
he'll look at me as if

I don't know a damn thing about living.
Sixth generation on his land, he understands
true ownership is wrought from work, not bought
or given as a hand-me-down.

If I ask him about the turds he's likely to say,
Sure, take what you need–
use my pick-up if you want.
And if I insult him with an offer to pay

he'll smile, forgiving my foolishness:
There'll come a time I'll need to call on you.
That's the way it is out here:
We call it country equity.

A Second Coming

Rough beast, you've come again, this time
on Easter morning. A cross between
the devil and his cur, your mottled fur's
a Jackson Pollack in his fiercest mood,

angst-sprinkled black and brown
with scarlet spackles where what you bit
bit back. If you're an omen, it's not
of some benign and easy born-again revival,

but grief gone crazy, anarchy dancing.
What hurt did you come from, what
haunted house? We tell ourselves
we are too old for this. You jump

and slobber, follow us everywhere,
eat and eat. We take you to the vet for shots.
Stronger now, you chase whatever moves:
grasshoppers, squirrels, the ring-tailed cat.

You pounce, flush doves from the field,
ducks from the pond. Even the loud-mouthed goose
retreats to deep water, pouts beyond your thrashing.
Who can tell you you'll never catch a deer,

that the white tail will always disappear
behind the juniper? Whatever we try to bury
you dig up, death on your breath. We tend
your wounds, they harden into scars.

Sit, we beg, but you will not. We coax and pat,
and when you're good, reward with treats. Eventually
you learn to stay. We name you Buddy, give you a collar
with a tag that says you're ours.

Thanksgiving

We stay in bed past ten, lying close,
the blanket pulled to block the light.
You are for me, and I for you, a family.

At breakfast wild turkeys cross the field,
inviting us out.
Brimming after weeks of rain

the lake reaches up to take us
into its deep abundance. Insect
darts for insect, the fish not far

behind, lunging and swallowing
just in time for the kingfisher to swipe
an instant three-course meal. On the far shore

four mergansers startle and fly, their
black wings drumming. It's afternoon already
when rain sends us inside. What shall I feed you,

this day of feasts? Leftovers, warmed while you shower.
We'll eat at the table by the window.
In the field the doe leads her fawn to his supper.

The sun, before it goes, tastes every tree on the hill,
lingering as if it will never have its fill.

Midsummer in the Blue Ridge

The rain has made a river of the road, beaten
the Joe-Pye weed into obedience.
Despite the weather
I go out, taking the path where it turns
at the potter's house, making my way
up the muddy hill
past the cabin where the white dog
languishes on the broken porch,
through the thicket of pale jewelweed,
pokeberry, and the flower
they call "live-for-ever".

Someone has cleared the graveyard
of summer's excess, and here,
in what should be a botanist's dream
of genus and species,
plastic flowers bloom at each grave:
fake red and pink, an eerie, everlasting green
against the fading names and dates.

The door to the church is open.
Only the locals know how long it's been
since the old stove rattled and sang
but the place still smells of sweat and woodsmoke.
Songs for a Christian Life, its back
broken from years of service, lies open:

Time, like an ever-rolling stream
bears all its sons away
They fly, forgotten as a dream,
dies at the opening day.

Back at the cabin my supper
simmers over the electric eye.
I turn the heat down, the television on,
and pour a glass of wine.

I skip channels
until there's news of home.
I'll call before the night is over.
It's not too late to come, I'll say,

and the weather will get better.
There's an old church back in the woods:
You could see for yourself tomorrow.

Equinox

And now we start our sure tilt toward the sun,
    toward galaxies of dandelions in
        the grass, whose every sun-drunk, wind-crazed blade's
          a dandy lying down for love, whose weeds

go wild, shoot for the sky; toward day's long run
    for gold, the great high-hurdle for abandon;
        flying with the grasshopper's leap, full tilt,
          leg-up, a crazy catapult, all out

for spring; toward meadowlarks sent up like sparks
    in sun-blanched, waist-high grass through which we walk—
        old flames, imagining our quick wild fire
          if we can hold on another summer.

III.

The Gift

Sunlight,
that time of day,
could make things speak.
I heard what I saw
in its slanting reach—
insistent, golden—
heard each piece of gravel in the street
announce itself for a shining instant
and then go silent.
It must have been autumn,
for I remember the catalpa tree with its yellow
leaves barely hanging on. It was 1954,
I was six, a girl on the sidewalk
in Charlotte, North Carolina.
I stood there watching the sun
slip behind the house across the street.
The whole world glowed as if
for one last time.
I remember wondering
why I had been given this—
why *I* was *I*—
when I heard the leaves speak
in tongues of dying light:

> *Look, quick, before*
> *we all go down.*

I took the gift inside but kept it
secret, for who would understand?

> *It's suppertime,* my mother said,
> *your turn to set the table.*

The Night Toboggan

On the lip
   of the long blind run
      everybody's backslapping brave

but me: a southern girl
   at the edge of womanhood
      a thousand miles from home.

This is the top of something
   nobody knows the bottom of,
      all of us myopic

in the new-moon night. Now
   in the last sweet
      instant of stability

I resign myself to snow—
   a numb, slow-frozen dying.
      We're off and flying

through icy air
   emptied of everything
      but sheer astonishment.

The end comes sooner
   than I'd guessed. I lie
      in darkness, the hill's heart

pumping all around me.
   A certain order penetrates the scene
      that wasn't there before:

trees reach, black vessels
    sprouting capillaries to the sky.
        Sky grows to snow

and snow to me,
    inseparably. Some delicate
        discreet reticulum moves

in and out and over me:
    this is the web of something
        nobody knows the secret of.

They're up the slope for another run.
    I stay below, listening as they come down
        shrieking, ripping into snow.

Snow

Do you see
how it loves this world,
how completely it embraces
the most neglected places,
like the empty space
between the wheelbarrow
and the house,

which only this morning
was nothing
but is now
a sparkling fullness,

how it flies
in the face of worry
with its steadfast grace,
its refusal to hurry,

how it comes
and keeps coming,
taking everything it wants—
field and tree,
house, hill and town—

how when it stops
it has no regrets
for what's left
untouched?

On the Road

I want to say
Leave me here,
you go on.

I am beginning to see
at night
the red meanderings
of the superhighways

mapped on the insides
of my eyes. I dream
I am building a wall around myself
of my old paperbacks:

Don't knock,
she's not at home.

I have lost my jacket,
my blue socks,
the good brush. July

is half gone. Which box
in what basement
did I leave the snow poem in?

Fireflies

They sparkle in the darkening field,
a thousand little inspirations. Sooner or later
you're bound to catch one
and when you do, you'll hold it
in your hand just long enough
to remember what you already know:

that you can't hold onto magic,
that it needs to keep moving, so you let it go,
but later in your room you're still after it,
bent over your desk, pen to paper.
The word you reach for fires and fades,
a glimmer of gold, a quick wild thing,

and once you've caught it, isn't
what you saw at all. Are you a fool? Of course.
But what if fireflies feed on your amazement,
if they need you as much as you need them?
You could do worse than to be a fool forever.
Go back to the field, my friend.

In That Other World

In that other world
there were more of them than any other bird,

billions in migration blocking the sun.
A single oak might hold a hundred nests,

so we cut down trees to get to them.
We ate them three meals a day.

Our wagon loads poured into market.
In that other world we shot the last wild flock

for pig feed, in one day
doing in a quarter million.

Martha, the last Passenger Pigeon,
died in the Cincinnati Zoo.

We froze her in a block of ice,
sent her to the Smithsonian

stuffed and mounted, where
those red eyes could stare out

forever,
for the world to come.

Remembering the Parrot of Carolina

You were a favorite
of the millinery trade,

your quill feathers yellow,
giving way to green, then blue,

bright orange at the shoulder.
If taken alive you could be tamed

in two days but were extremely
mischievous in orchards.

If one of you was shot
the whole flock swept repeatedly

around its dead companion.
This is what they say about you in the old book:

The gun was kept continually at work
and at each successive shot,
though showers of them fell,
the affection of the survivors
increased.

Verge of Extinction

Already gone, the Iberian lynx,
Brazil's guitarfish and South Africa's
national flower. Gone, too, the Scottish
crossbill, the parrot of Carolina.
Almost gone, the trees at Kew hanging on
in a greenhouse, their lucky progeny
stored in a seed bank we name Millenium.
Meanwhile, talk's cheap and money's always money.
We argue over global warming and complain
about the price of gas; revise, re-think;
waiting for more evidence of ruin than
twelve thousand species or more on the brink.
Busy sawing off the limb we stand on,
we miss the news of our own oblivion.

Continued

Floater

Bat out of hell,
she followed me
as I drove to my friend
the ophthalmologist,
black wings flapping
against the rear-view mirror.
She'd come out of nowhere,
wriggling across my field of vision
and now she was everywhere:
the bedroom ceiling,
the page of the book,
the sky.

The problem, he said,
was in the vitreous, surgery
too risky. In time
I would learn to live with it.
He gave me a prescription
for thicker glasses
and hugged a casual goodbye.

A month later he lay down
in his driveway,
put a gun in his mouth
and pulled the trigger.

I close my eyes and try
to imagine him looking up
for the last time
at the sky. What vision
haunted him, made him crave
an end to sight?

When I open my eyes again
she's there—blackbird
flailing against her cage,
black fly battering
the inside of the window.
She's with me always,
everywhere,
her shifting shape
flickering even in my sleep.

Rising

All night while they slept
the water was rising
and as they sat at breakfast
with coffee and croissants

it was rising
while they bent over desks
in their important offices
the water rose and kept rising

as they met after work for drinks
(gin and tonic, a good chardonnay)
though they knew it was rising
they ordered another drink

and drove home through water
still rising He said *I think it's starting
to go down* She said *Surely someone
will tell us if we ought to leave*

The children called from faraway
to say *We've seen it on TV*
She said *We're fine* although by then
the water was up to the windowsills

They ate their dinner by candlelight
and went to sleep, sure that tomorrow someone
would rescue them and they would be
as safe and happy as they had always been.

Drought

We hunker down against the heat,
close the curtains, shut the blinds.
We live our lives inside: we say
this can't go on forever.

We eat too much, go on a diet,
play cards, peruse the catalogues,
pay bills, flip through old magazines.
Take sleepless naps. Late afternoon,

when thunder shakes the floor
and sends a shiver down the walls,
we huddle in bed and celebrate the cool,
charged air, but when the storm is over

we lie together in our pool of sweat
more parched than ever. You turn the TV on,
click past the latest Baghdad bombings
to the local weather. I close my eyes.

You should know better, my sweet,
than to keep hoping for a break in the heat.

Reversal

The only way to see the world
may be to turn it upside down,
as when at five or six you lay
on your back on the sofa

and walked across the ceiling
stepping across the tops of doors
onto the white plain
of your imagination

or when you lie beside me,
sky filling creek, moon
floating on its back
in the warm brackish bath.

Look: the heron who disappears
behind the drowning marsh grass
rises only by forgetting
her uprightness.

Red

December: a feeble sun
and the kind of cold that steals
through quilt and flannel, intent
on taking up a winter residence
in the bones. Is it
the morning's uncertain light
that makes me wonder how I got here—
to this last month of a year
with a futuristic sound,
to this house on a hill
in the middle of nowhere, to the bed
I share with a man who's not
my children's father, to my 60th year
with this gray stranger—myself—
in the mirror?

I stir the coals in the woodstove,
shove my bare feet into my boots and zip
my jacket over my pajamas. Outside
I spread the seed I've brought for the birds
and linger at the edge of the yard
where the cliff drops down to the creek.
The sound I hear isn't an answer
but it tells me how
to let the questions go.
I'm turning back to the house content
to let the day settle into a comfortable grayness,
into quiet gratitude, when I see them
in the highest branches—robins, hundreds of them,
their urgent warbling louder than the rush below.
I take a measure of their song inside,
into the bed, where we hold each other,
the day dawning all over again:

so red, so red.

IV.

My Father As Zookeeper

Dead now twenty years, he zooms
into my dream, his glasses broken,
the drab green uniform
swallowing him.

Don't worry, he says,
I've brought my whip,
but by now the elephants are out,
the wind from their great flapping ears

has shaken the monkey house down
and the chimpanzees
are hurling bananas
from the trees.

The leopard is nowhere
to be found, though the parrots say
she's holding the west end of town
and painting spots on the cathedral dome.

Hours pass while my father
chases the old idea of order. Not until sundown
does he give up, exhaustion closing in.
He tries his whip as a walking stick, he falls,

he moans: *Is this the someday you warned me about?*
the day the revolution comes?

Hush, I say,
and take him in my arms.

Menopause

Three in the morning: I wake
in the rain forest that is my room.
Huge tropical vines reach out for me,
heavy with the fruit of my myopia,
its maroon juices dripping
from the ceiling, down the walls.

What am I doing here?
I've sworn to give up traveling
to dangerous places.
Is the water drinkable?
And what of these faces peering at me
through the curtain of leaves?

My sweat is a river
sucking me
into its heart of darkness.
I see a vision of my hair
gone white, my face
without its flesh.

I close my eyes.
It's almost morning
when I step out onto dry land,
onto the field of middle age
where I find my glasses,
my familiar life.

In the Country of the Young

In the theater off Harvard Square
the sum of all their arms is more
than twice each darkened head—

hundreds of arms, some long and thin
and tensed in the hard pursuit of touch,
some heavy with listless energy—

arm into arm, hand into hand,
they reproduce until the whole house
is held in one embrace. Never mind

the movie—Antonioni, *St. Matthew's
Passion,* Bach's crackling soundtrack.
Never mind the old man who sits

behind them, last row at the back,
Professor Emeritus of something
ancient and irrelevant, whose hands

find only each other, lie one against
the other, like two old lovers napping
in the country of the young.

Advice We Give Our Children

goes in one ear and out the other, goes
where the wild things are, somewhere mid-air be-
tween wise and wry surprise, as if it knows
the way by heart; courts serendipity,
crosses the street without holding hands,
ignores entreaties and prefers the ne'er
do well to well-to-do, tries contraband,
gets high and sobers up— until we swear
we'll give up giving it. What, after all,
do *we* know? And yet it seems we've done quite
well, made parents proud, despite our refusal
to listen. Amazing, how we learned right
from wrong, butt-headed as we've always been.
Who better, then, to give advice to children?

His Father

wakes to find himself alive again,
the bedroom thickly dark except
for the luminous green of the clock,
both hands hanging on six,

but a.m. and p.m. have long ago
stopped mattering. Outside
(or is it inside?) a smattering of talk,
some meanness in it, a woman

who might have been his wife, a boy
who'd got her pregnant, who just might be
the same as he whose broken body he finds himself
inhabiting. The old dog's bark

gnaws the room's rank air. Who
feeds the dead? Do the dead still need?
He resolves to get up,
take a piss, and look for answers.

The Lions

Lions make bad pets, my mother e-mails,
as if I'd said I wanted one, *and there
are more in Texas than in any other state.*

Before this I had not thought of lions
in a year, and then only on PBS,
the aerial view of a pride on the run,

a zoom to the elegant head as it spies its kill.
They know instinctively, she writes,
when small children are near,

and then: *Be careful.* Is this the first spark
of her brain shorting out? Her grandchildren
are grown, with lives of their own nowhere

near Texas. Perhaps she shouldn't live alone.
I won't reply except to say I'll visit soon.
But nights, now, the lions watch me

from their lush green blind.
Do they smell my scent, admixture
of envy and fear? When they turn to run

I tremble at the fierceness
of such grace. Soon they are gone.
They were so lovely and so young.

Looking Out

All day the ocean reaches and resigns,
waves heaving towards the burning beach
then hissing into slow retreat.

Each wave's a lesson we won't learn,
who build our castles in the sand
like children who believe in fortresses

but miss the message in the roar:
Is it that death is something like desire?
Over decades the water's yin and yang

obliterates a row of houses and a street.
We build them back as if we mean to stay,
and where dunes used to be, we stand knee-deep,

toes digging in, looking out. We can't stop looking,
loving with something like abandon
the sea that sucks away the sand we stand on.

Coquinas

Here, at the intersection
of land and ocean, from the salty
potion of plankton and seawater
we suck our sustenance.

Where the Atlantic lets go
its striving and its grief—
those liquid muscles
loosening into a kind of peace—

we bury ourselves alive.
How we love to dive
into the dark belly
of the beach.

Television

I hate the passionate talking heads talking terror
I hate the blood and the body parts
the indisputable black and white of the documentaries
the easy answers and the refusals to answer
I hate the 10 o'clock local news
the drunks driving the wrong way down the interstate
the athletes opining as if a football game were World War III
I hate how the late-night newsladies feel compelled to look foxy
I hate how the anchormen won't sit at a desk anymore
I hate that I want to win at Jeopardy
I hate hunting between the sheets for the lost remote
I hate the smugness of the woman who's invested wisely
and wants to sell me an annuity
who doesn't know or care what came just before:
the swollen bellies of the babies in Darfur
I hate the weather, the weather, the weather
dew point and wind chill and variance from average rainfall
in North Dakota
I hate that there's nothing to watch on any of 600 channels
I hate what I pay for cable
I hate the preacher promising salvation and how I want to listen
I hate how the TV talks me to sleep
how its stupidity settles me
I hate the thought that it might be my last companion
the thought of myself sitting in front of it
at eighty or ninety
my mind mostly gone but hostage
to this dumbed-down loud-mouthed abuser
who thinks just because I don't leave it
I don't hate it

1-800-RU-n-PAIN

Thank you for calling!
You're no longer alone!
We're here to feel your pain
and make you whole again.
Press 1 if you ache in the small of your back.
Press 2 if your head hurts when you think.
For all other bodily parts in pain
press 3. For existential angst,
malaise and anomie, press 4.
For religious doubt press 5, and 6
for fear of dying. Choose 7 if your spouse
has left you, 8 if your children ignore you.
If your pain defies description, press 9.
Thank you for sharing your pain!
Remember, we will make you whole again.
No fee until recovery! And if we decide the law
won't right your wrong we'll help you find
the perfect match from our nationwide panel
of experienced and caring therapists.
We accept all major credit cards!
Thank you for calling 1-800-RU-n-PAIN!
Tell a friend! And if you enroll
in the month of October
we have a special offer—
A prime-time interview
and a published memoir
for the winning sufferer!

Black Friday

On the biggest day of the shopping year
I fight for my faraway parking place,
resolved once more to be a better buyer.

I have to steel myself to leave the car,
to keep my pace in the furious race
on this biggest shopping day of the year,

to be the Purchaser Extraordinaire,
the Queen of the Mall with the poker face,
resolved anew to be a better buyer.

Inside the store I wonder what's the matter,
why nothing on the clearance rack comes close,
on this biggest shopping day of the year,

to covering the ass in the three-way mirror.
How long have they trained for this effortless
grace, these resolute buyers, my betters?

When it's over I hunt for my lost car
in a sea of steel; humbly taking my place
in the worst traffic of the shopping year,
resolved, next time to be a better buyer.

This Body

These breasts
won't buy a miracle bra

They are too pleased with themselves
to be pushed around

This ass
doesn't fit in designer jeans

It's full of itself
and entirely satisfied

This skin
won't wear perfume,

its scent's the sweat and lust
of half a century

This body
doesn't wear any furs except

its own almost-ermine skullcap,
its little gray fox at the pubis

The Loop

On the loop between ought and ought not
I go jogging past the doughnut shop,
my lungs heaving on the grease-heavy air,
my feet struggling to stay on course. I hear

familiar voices in my head, the old debate:
You only live once, says the reprobate,
a hefty, jolly girl, to her anorectic twin;
and in reply, *Do not give in!*

I stop, propose a compromise, which they
reluctantly accept. Again we're on our way.
I circle one more time, my run
reduced to limping walk, and turn

where heavenly aromas emanate
from the open door. I call it Fate,
this smiling face which offers sweet profusion.
No slave to choice, I settle for half a dozen.

Prayer

Back then I knelt on knobby knees, my palms
together, fingers pointing towards the sky
where I'd been taught God lived, his cosmic arms
ready to take me in if I should die
before I waked. Believe me when I say
that what I wanted most was to believe.
Before I lay me down to sleep I'd pray
forgiveness for sins I couldn't conceive—
the Devil's most determined wickedness
had yet to work on me. Now, near sixty,
my heaven is this bed, my holiness
this slow fire of flesh on flesh. Love, let me
perfect these imperfections until at last
I give the worms their host, their hard-earned feast.

Understudy

What the old one's singing you can't hear
unless you lean down, your head
on her chest, unless

you hold your breath as her heart
finds the beat of the blues or
a Bach cantata. Put your ear

to her lips and listen: *Swing low*
I'm dreaming of a white
Here comes the sun

Lie down beside her.
Before too long
you'll be called on to sing her song.

To the Young Man of Middle Eastern Descent at Gate 13, London to New York

You sit across from me picking your nails,
your right hand working on your left,
then left on right until you dig a jewel of blood

from the quick. Dark glasses hide your eyes,
but I imagine them deep-set and brooding.
Your lips move, words lost in the loudspeaker's drone:

first class and parents with small children.
Now your fingers cease their fidgeting, touch
palm to palm. A prayer? Unnaturally erect,

you sit with your back to the window, the red
dawn falling around your shoulders like a shawl.
You seem immune to noise and swirl, already

in a world beyond our worldliness. *Rows 40
through 20.* Relax, I tell myself, and yet...what's wrong
with caution, common sense? What's lost

if I report you? *Last call to board.* You stand, and only then
I see the wire that wends its way from your ear to the little box
you keep your music in. You're no satan, no saint,

only a guy waiting in line, at best a minor angel in a host
of ambiguities. Wherever you're going, we're going with you,
all of us rising on our shared pair of wings.

Creed

If you ask me what I believe in,

it is the body of the ninety year old
straining to stand upright, each vertebra
a testament, each muscle a miracle.

It is the shape of her head,
a sculpture the artist
has been working on for centuries,

the skull visible
under the veil of skin;
and if you ask me for a sermon

I will give you that skin,
every wrinkle a parable.
If you insist upon sacrament

I say take her hand in yours:
it is the only way to save yourself.
Fold your flesh into her bones

until you do not have to ask me anymore
what to believe in:
It is the body

the body,

Amen.

Notes

"Verge of Extinction": The last two lines of this poem are based on a quote from Paul Erlich: "In pushing other species to extinction, humanity is busy sawing off the limb on which it is perched."

My information about the now-extinct Carolina Parakeet and Passenger Pigeon is taken from Catesby's *Birds of Colonial America*, edited by Alan Feduccia, University of North Carolina Press, 1985.

"Mid-Summer in the Blue Ridge": the hymn stanza is from *O God, Our Help in Ages Past,* by Isaac Watts

About the Author

Photo by Luke Robinson

Lee Robinson's first collection of poetry, *Hearsay*, won the 2003 Poets Out Loud Prize from Fordham University Press as well as the Texas Writers League Violet Crown Award. She is also the author of a novel for young adults, *Gateway* (Houghton Mifflin). She practiced law for 25 years in South Carolina and now teaches at the Center for Medical Humanities and Ethics, University of Texas Health Science Center at San Antonio. She lives with her husband, physician/writer Jerald Winakur, in Comfort, Texas.

www.ingramcontent.com/pod-product-compliance
Lightning Source LLC
Chambersburg PA
CBHW071839290426
44109CB00017B/1868